NUTRITION
What's in the Food We Eat

DOROTHY HINSHAW PATENT

photographs by William Muñoz

Holiday House/New York

The author and photographer wish to thank the following people for helping with this book: Dan Vonique; Dyshauntic and Damailiyha Bletson; Gabriel and Miguel Borges; Jerry Chen; Carla Cox; Holly, Amber, and Jonel Finley; Sean Muñoz; Charlotte Powell; John Thomas; and Amelia and Mary Ellen Wood

Library of Congress Cataloging-in-Publication Data
Patent, Dorothy Hinshaw.
Nutrition : what's in the food we eat / Dorothy Hinshaw Patent ;
photos by William Muñoz.
p.   cm.
Summary: Explains how different types of foods provide nutrients
for the body.
ISBN 0-8234-0968-6
1. Nutrition—Juvenile literature. [1. Nutrition.] I. Muñoz,
William, ill. II. Title.
QP141.P355   1992
612.3—dc20
92–3665   CIP   AC

For all the mothers who prepare healthy, wonderful food for their children, especially those who did so for this book

D.H.P.

Contents

CHAPTER ONE

What Food Does for Us

Why do we need to eat? We get hungry, and we enjoy eating. But what does food do for us? Among other things, food gives us energy. Our bodies need energy all the time. Even when we are sitting still, we are using energy. Our hearts need energy to beat. Our brains need energy to think. And when we move, even by just blinking an eyelid, our muscles use up energy.

Food also provides the things our bodies need for growth. Energy is used to turn the protein from food into muscles. Calcium helps make new bones. Other food substances are also needed for growth.

If we get hurt, our bodies use the energy and materials gained from food to heal.

We can see the outside of our body renewing itself as our hair and nails grow. The inside of our body is constantly renewing itself as well.

Even grown-ups need the things in food that help growth. That's because living things are always renewing themselves, constantly breaking down old parts and replacing them with new ones. In this way, our bodies wear out only slowly, even though we are using them all the time.

Beans, grains, and dried fruit
are rich sources of the nutrients
our bodies need.

The word *nutrition* means what is in our food and how it
is used inside us. Everything we eat is made up of a variety of
chemicals. Those our bodies use are called *nutrients*.

This girl is eating a vegetarian pita sandwich, a food from the Middle East.

Our bodies are wonderful chemical factories. They take in food, change it chemically, and turn it into parts of ourselves. When we swallow the food, it goes to our stomachs, then to our small intestines. Starting in the mouth, the chemicals in what we eat are broken down into smaller chemicals. These are taken into our blood, which carries them to where they are needed.

The cells of the body use some of the chemicals as building blocks for making new parts. Other chemicals are used to provide energy. In the meantime, what we don't use passes into the large intestine. There, water is removed. Then what's left passes out in our feces.

Mexican foods such as tostadas and enchiladas can be healthful as long as they aren't made with too much fat.

CHAPTER TWO

Carbohydrates Mean Energy

Most of our food is made up of sugar, starches, and other carbohydrates. These foods provide energy our body needs. The word *calorie* is a measure of energy. When we say something we eat has a lot of calories, we mean that it can provide us with plenty of energy.

Simple sugar, such as white table sugar, is the quickest energy source. We can use it right away. Other carbohydrates, like the starch in potatoes or spaghetti, must be changed into sugar by the body before they can be used. That doesn't mean you should eat or drink heavily sweetened foods. Sugar gets used up quickly. The energy in starches lasts longer, since it takes the body longer to break the starches down.

All of these foods are high in carbohydrates.

Sugary candies like these have no nutritional value except for the calories in the sugar.

There's another problem with sugary foods and drinks. When we guzzle down regular soft drinks, we are getting a lot of sugar calories. But the soft drink gives us only "empty calories," with no other benefits. If we eat fresh oranges, however, the sugar calories come along with other things our bodies need, like vitamin C and fiber.

When we need quick energy, fruit is a good thing to eat. Not only does fruit provide us with more than just sugar calories, but it also tastes delicious. Dried fruits make especially satisfying quick snacks.

Starches are found in a variety of foods. Potatoes, rice, and pasta like spaghetti and macaroni contain lots of starch. The starch in these foods comes with B vitamins and other things our bodies need.

Vegetables such as carrots, broccoli, tomatoes, and corn contain both sugars and starches. Like fruits and potatoes, these vegetables bring vitamins and other important chemicals into our diet.

Different kinds of pasta

Garden vegetables

CHAPTER THREE

Protein Builds Bodies

In America, we eat plenty of meat. Meat is one of the best sources of protein. Protein is not only needed for muscles; it also makes up most of the other parts of our bodies, such as our livers and brains. It gives our bodies their covering, forming our skin, hair, and nails. The tendons that connect muscles to bone and the cartilage that cushions bones where they meet are also made of protein. So is the living part of bone.

Meat from beef cattle like these is rich in protein.

These foods are high in protein.

Protein is made up of building blocks called *amino acids*. Each protein molecule is a chain of amino acids strung together. Our bodies need 22 different amino acids. We can make 14, but the other 8 must come in our food. They are called *essential amino acids*. Foods like eggs, milk, and meat contain the essential amino acids in the right amounts for our bodies. These foods are said to contain *complete protein*.

Soup with pasta, beans, and other vegetables provides plenty of protein.

Some people eat only non-meat foods. They are called vegetarians. How do they get enough protein in their diet? Actually, that isn't difficult. Some vegetarians will eat eggs and cheese and drink milk. That way, non-meat eaters get plenty of protein.

Other vegetarians won't eat any food that comes from the animal kingdom. They eat only plant foods, so they don't drink milk or eat eggs. But they still can get enough protein to be healthy. How? Vegetable foods, especially those that come from the seeds of plants, such as grains, corn, and beans, contain quite a bit of protein. In these foods, some of the essential amino acids are present only in small quantities. For that reason, our bodies can only use part of the protein.

Different plant foods are low in different amino acids. For example, if we ate just beans, we wouldn't get much usable protein. But if we combined the beans with wheat, say, by eating a couple of pieces of whole wheat toast with our baked beans, we would get a good quantity of complete protein. The wheat would make up for the amino acids that are low in the beans and vice versa.

Beans and grains together provide complete protein.

CHAPTER FOUR

Storing Up Food: Fat

These days, *fat* seems to be a bad word. It's true that most Americans eat too much of it. Butter, margarine, and the oil used to fry foods are just about pure fat, which means concentrated calories. That's important for people who work hard at physical labor. But most Americans nowadays work sitting at desks, not chopping up firewood or plowing fields. Even children today spend more time sitting than their parents did when they were young.

Logging with horses the old-fashioned way is gentle on the environment. It also burns lots of calories.

For many people, computer games and television are now the main form of entertainment and play. That means today's children are less active, and therefore need fewer calories to keep healthy.

In a way, fat is like sugar. It can contain important nutrients, such as vitamin E. But there are so many calories and so few other nutrients in it that most fat calories are empty, like those in sugar. It's much better to fill energy needs with foods rich in vitamins, like fresh fruits and vegetables, than with greasy ones, such as fried foods. If we eat too much fat, we can add fat to our bodies and still not get enough other nutrients.

Deep-fried foods are loaded with fat.

21

Just one serving of salad dressing gives us enough fat for a whole day.

Fats are important in the body. They form part of the membranes that surround each body cell. A thin layer of fat under the skin helps keep the body warm. Muscles contain some fat, which provides them with energy to do work. And the oils in our skin help keep it healthy.

We actually need only a little fat each day—equal to about a tablespoon of vegetable oil. It's easy to get that small amount—just the dressing on a large salad has about that much, and even broiled lean meat contains some fat. We only need a little fat because our bodies can make most of their building blocks from proteins and carbohydrates.

Too much of the wrong kind of fat can cause damage to our hearts and blood vessels. Fat from animals is most likely to cause trouble. Meat, eggs, butter, cream, and cheese all contain animal fats. Eating a lot of such foods can result in too much of a chemical called *cholesterol* (ko-LESS-ter-all) in the blood. Cholesterol can be deposited on the inside of artery walls. This makes the passageways through these vessels narrower. After many years, there can be so much cholesterol deposited that the blood can no longer flow through the vessels. When this happens to an artery supplying the heart, a heart attack is the result.

These foods are all high in fat.

Frozen yogurt is delicious and has less fat than ice cream.

It's not hard to control how much fat we eat. We can avoid fried foods, drink low-fat or skim milk, and eat small amounts of red meat and rich desserts. Instead of French fries, we can have a baked potato with a little margarine. We can eat broiled chicken without the skin instead of fried chicken. We can treat ourselves to frozen yogurt instead of ice cream.

CHAPTER FIVE

A Little Goes a Long Way: Vitamins and Minerals

Vitamins and minerals are powerful nutrients. We need them in only small amounts in our diets. Yet if we don't get enough of them, we can become sick.

Vitamins play a special role in our health. They form parts of some of the important chemicals called *enzymes* (EN-zimes). Enzymes are the workhorses of our chemical factories. There are many different enzymes in the body. Without them, our complicated chemistry would not work right. But since we need only a little bit of each kind of enzyme, we don't need large amounts of vitamins.

We need at least 13 different vitamins. If we eat plenty of vegetables, fruits, and grains, we get most of the vitamins we need. Oranges, green beans, broccoli, and whole grain bread are good sources for many vitamins.

Fresh garden fruits and vegetables contain a variety of vitamins.

All of these vegetables and fruits contain plenty of vitamin A.

We can get vitamin A from dairy products such as milk and from liver. Vitamin A is also made by our bodies from a chemical called carotene, found in orange, yellow, and dark green vegetables. Vitamin A is important for healthy skin and for clear breathing. It helps our eyes see in dim light, too.

Eight vitamins are grouped together as B vitamins. Most of them are found in meat. But some are also common in different kinds of vegetables. Each B vitamin has its own special role in our bodies.

Vitamin C is abundant in fruits such as oranges and grapefruit. Broccoli and tomatoes also have a lot of vitamin C. Vitamin C is important for strong bones and teeth and helps our bodies fight germs.

Vitamin D is unusual. Our bodies can make it when sunlight strikes our skin. But people with dark skins who live in cold climates and people who spend most of their time indoors need vitamin D in their diets. They can get it from milk with added vitamin D, fish such as tuna and salmon, and egg yolks. Vitamin D is needed for strong bones.

Citrus fruits such as lemons, grapefruits, oranges, and limes are high in vitamin C.

Nuts are rich in vitamin E.

Vitamin E helps to protect red blood cells, which carry oxygen to the body's cells. It is found in vegetable oils, nuts, and wheat germ.

We don't hear much about vitamin K, since getting it is easy. Bacteria living in our intestines can make it. Vitamin K helps the body produce materials involved in blood clotting when we are injured. It also helps keep bones healthy.

Our bodies require small amounts of a number of minerals, called *trace elements*. Most of them are needed in such tiny quantities that they are easy to get by eating a balanced diet.

One trace element that we sometimes lack is iron. We need iron to make the chemical in red blood cells that carries oxygen to our body's cells. Without enough iron, we can tire easily, feel weak, and look pale. Red meat, whole grain cereals, and dried beans are good sources of iron.

Some minerals we need in larger amounts. Like the trace elements, most are easy to get in a balanced diet. But some people don't get enough calcium. Calcium is vital in building bones and teeth. It is also important for the normal workings of cells, including muscles. Milk, yogurt, sardines, canned salmon with the bones, dried beans, and dark green, leafy vegetables are good calcium sources.

Cooking in an iron skillet can increase our food's iron content.

CHAPTER SIX

Healthy Eating

Eating a healthy diet doesn't mean giving up favorite foods. Pizza, for example, can be a healthy food if it's made the right way. A hand-tossed pizza has less fat than a deep-dish one. To make a deep-dish pizza, lots of fat is put in the pan to produce a crisp crust and to keep it from sticking. What goes on top of the pizza also makes a difference. Toppings such as mushrooms, green peppers, and pineapple are good for you and fat-free. Pepperoni and sausage, however, have lots of fat.

The topping on this pizza includes peppers, mushrooms, olives, and cauliflower.

Eating a well-balanced meal makes you feel good.

When you eat at a fast-food restaurant, choose a sandwich made with broiled chicken breast instead of a hamburger or a fried fish sandwich. Have a salad instead of French fries. And choose low-fat milk or fruit juice rather than a milk shake or a soft drink.

In general, the fresher the food, the better. Packaged foods that have undergone lots of processing, like potato chips and TV dinners, often have loads of fat and salt added. Vitamins, minerals, and fiber usually are reduced when foods are highly processed.

We are very lucky in America. We can buy many kinds of fresh foods year-round. A banana or an apple can be a satisfying after-school snack. Carrot sticks or green-pepper strips add variety to bag lunches.

These processed foods have fewer nutrients than fresh, unprocessed foods.

If you want a crunchy snack, choose to munch on pretzels rather than potato chips. Pretzels have very little fat, whereas potato chips are mostly fat. There are now tortilla chips that are baked instead of fried. They taste great dipped in salsa.

Television ads may try to make you think otherwise, but fresh, healthy foods can be delicious as well as good for you. When you eat the right diet, you will have more energy and will feel better than if you always feast on greasy hamburgers and potato chips.

Homemade Soft Pretzels

(Don't bake pretzels without an adult's permission.)

> 1 package active dry yeast
> 1½ cups warm water
> 1 tablespoon sugar
> 4 cups all-purpose flour
> 1 tablespoon salt
> 1 egg

Sprinkle the yeast over the warm water in a small bowl. Stir in the sugar. While the yeast dissolves, mix the flour and salt in a large bowl. Gradually add the flour to the yeast mixture and stir together to make a very stiff dough. You may not need to mix in all the flour.

Turn this mixture out onto a countertop and knead until the dough is smooth and no longer sticky.

Pinch off 12 balls of dough and roll each piece into a rope about 16 inches long. Shape into a pretzel. Place the pretzels about two inches apart on a large, lightly greased cookie sheet. When all the pretzels have been shaped, cover them loosely with a towel and set them aside while the oven heats up.

Place the oven rack in the center of the oven and preheat to 400°F. Beat the egg with a fork and brush it over the tops of the pretzels.

Bake about 15 minutes, or until pretzels are golden brown. Cool on racks. Fresh pretzels are best eaten while still warm.

Calories Burned by a 110-Pound Person in 30 Minutes of Activity

Card-playing	39
Piano playing	60
Running (8-minute mile)	324
Standing quietly	42
Swimming slow crawl	192
Table tennis	102
Volleyball	75
Walking, normal pace	120

Your body burns many more calories when you are physically active than when you are inactive.

Food Guide Pyramid
A Guide to Daily Food Choices

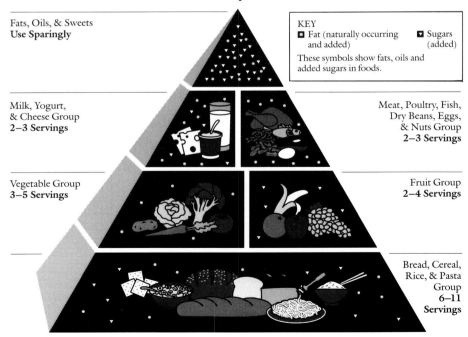

Fats, Oils, & Sweets
Use Sparingly

KEY
☐ Fat (naturally occurring and added)   ☑ Sugars (added)
These symbols show fats, oils and added sugars in foods.

Milk, Yogurt, & Cheese Group
2–3 Servings

Meat, Poultry, Fish, Dry Beans, Eggs, & Nuts Group
2–3 Servings

Vegetable Group
3–5 Servings

Fruit Group
2–4 Servings

Bread, Cereal, Rice, & Pasta Group
6–11 Servings

This food pyramid was recommended as a guideline to a healthy diet by the federal government in 1992.

Calories and Fat Content of Foods

(taken from the United States Department of Agriculture's publication, *Composition of Foods, Agricultural Handbook No. 8*, except for frozen yogurt, which is from nutritional information on the package)

Food and Quantity	Calories	% Fat*
Ice cream, *3 ounces*	177	54%
Frozen yogurt, *3 ounces*	110	36%
Potato chips, *1 ounce*	162	63%
Pretzels, *1 ounce*	111	10%
French fries, *20 pieces*	274	43%
Baked potato, *one plain*	186	1%
Regular hamburger, *3 ounces*	245	64%
Broiled chicken breast, *3 ounces*	142	18%
Fish sticks, *3 ounces*	151	46%
Broiled cod, *3 ounces*	146	28%
Whole milk, *1 cup*	149	48%
Skim milk, *1 cup*	82	2.5%

* "Percent fat" means percent of calories from fat. Calorie content and fat content of many foods will vary, depending on source, brand, and preparation.

Glossary

amino acids: The building blocks of protein. Our bodies can make 14 of the 22 we need but must get the other 8 from our food.

artery: A vessel that carries blood from the heart through the body.

calcium: A mineral in dairy products, dried beans, and dark green vegetables that we need for our bones.

calorie: A measure of the energy in food.

carbohydrates: Sugars and starches. Foods with lots of carbohydrates give us quick energy.

carotene: An orange chemical in foods like carrots that our bodies change into vitamin A.

cholesterol: A waxlike substance found in the animal foods we eat. Our bodies also make it.

energy: The capacity for doing work. Our bodies get energy from the food we eat.

enzymes: Products in the body that help chemical reactions take place.

fat: A type of nutrient containing concentrated calories.

feces: Waste products discharged by the body from the intestines.

fiber: Indigestible material in plant foods that is left over after digestion. Fiber is good for our bodies because it helps the intestines work well and helps prevent cancer.

minerals: Substances such as iron and calcium that our bodies extract from the food we eat.

nutrients: The substances in food that our bodies use.

nutrition: The science of nourishment; how our bodies are nourished by the food we eat.

processed food: Foods with ingredients that have been changed in factories to make them last longer without spoiling. Many important nutrients that our bodies need in small quantities may have been removed from processed foods.

protein: Chemicals made up of chains of amino acids that our bodies use to build muscles, skin, hair, and other important parts.

starches: Carbohydrates that are broken down into sugars before the body can use them.

sugars: Chemicals in food that the body can use for quick energy.

trace elements: Minerals our bodies need in small quantities.

vegetarian: A person who doesn't eat meat. Some vegetarians also avoid dairy products.

vitamins: Vital nutrients we need in small amounts.

Index